AUDUBON'S
BIRDS

WITH ILLUSTRATIONS BY
JOHN JAMES AUDUBON

WRITTEN BY
ROBERTA SEWAL

THE GROLIER SOCIETY INC. • NEW YORK

WILD TURKEY GOBBLER

THIS painting of the wild turkey is the most famous one John James Audubon did.

Wild turkeys are probably the finest game in the world. They are delicious to eat, especially if they have been fed on acorns, fruit and berries.

The male turkey is called a gobbler. The female is called a hen. The gobblers are much larger and more colorful than the hens.

These turkeys can fly at very fast speeds.

Wild turkeys spend most of their time on the ground in search of food. In the evening they fly into trees to roost.

You can see these wild turkeys in Pennsylvania and Oklahoma and in central Mexico. Mr. Audubon once saw a wild turkey that weighed thirty-six pounds and had a beard a foot long!

Male

BALTIMORE ORIOLE

THE male Baltimore oriole is one of North America's most beautiful songbirds. He has a bright orange breast, a black head, and an orange-and-black tail with spots of white.

These orioles like to build their nests in the topmost branches of elm or maple trees. You can see them on farms, in villages and parks, and on roadsides in the northeast part of the United States.

Orioles are insect-eating birds and are very valuable to man. Sometimes they will also eat fruit and berries.

It is interesting that the Baltimore oriole is likely to return each spring to the same neighborhood—sometimes to the very same tree! —after a winter spent as far away as Peru or Colombia in South America.

1 and 2 Males; 3 Female and nest

MOURNING DOVE

THIS bird gets its name from its deep sorrowful call. It is found throughout most of the United States.

The mourning dove eats seeds. One dove can eat as many as 7,500 small seeds in a few hours!

This dove is noisy when it flies. Its wings seem to whistle. Have you ever heard a whistle from the sky? Perhaps you heard a mourning dove.

The mourning dove does not build strong nests. They are very loosely woven and last barely long enough for the eggs to hatch.

You usually see mourning doves in pairs. The male and female stay together most of the time. These doves fly south in the winter, and they gather in large flocks.

1 Male; 2 Female

9

PAINTED BUNTING

Few wild birds of North America wear such a variety of gorgeous colors as the mature male bunting. Its colors are beautiful: blue-violet, red, scarlet, and yellow-green.

Painted buntings used to be captured and sold as pets. They are as attractive for their song as for their appearance. These little birds were caught by setting a cage with a stuffed male bunting in an open space. The real male bunting would try to attack the stuffed one and end up by getting trapped in the cage.

These birds are located in the southern part of the United States. They seldom come further north than North Carolina.

Painted buntings prefer thickets, hedgerows and the shrubbery of city gardens. Their food is weed and grain seed, worms and weevils and other small insects.

Even people who have had the chance of seeing a painted bunting at close view, thrill each time they see these brilliant birds and hear its sweet song.

1 and 2 Old Males; 3 Male of 1st Year; 4 2nd Year; 5 Female

11

BELTED KINGFISHER

WITH its big head and crest and blue back, the belted kingfisher is not easily mistaken for any other bird. Both sexes wear a blue collar but the female also has a chestnut band across her white breast, as shown by the bird swallowing a fish in Audubon's plate. Its voice sounds like a rattling party noise-maker.

These kingfisher are found by lakes and watercourses. In the summer they are located throughout most of the United States. In the winter they fly south to South America.

They eat small fish. The kingfisher's spearlike, powerful beak is useful for fishing. When fish are scarce, mice, frogs, insects and even fruit are also taken.

1 and 2 Male; 3 Female

WHIPPOORWILL

THIS songbird is named for its loud three-syllable call. You will know it right away, even if you never heard it. It whistles over and over again: Whip-poor-Will! Probably a thousand people have *heard* the whippoorwill for every one who has ever seen it.

During the summer the whippoorwill spends all night whistling so loud that it can be heard half a mile away. Sometimes it repeats its note more than a thousand times without stopping!

This is a slim bird with a large head and a huge, whiskered mouth that can swallow even the largest moths. It eats mosquitoes, grasshoppers and many other insects.

These birds live in woods and thickets in the northern part of the United States.

1 Male; 2 and 3 Female

14

15

BROAD-WINGED HAWK

THERE are many broad-winged hawks in the forests of North America. It is one of the most helpful birds to mankind.

This hawk eats rats and mice as well as snakes, frogs and large insects.

Sometimes the broad-winged hawk will sit for hours on a shaded branch of a tree waiting for some of his food to come along. Because of this, Mr. Audubon called these hawks "quiet, tame and rather inactive."

The broad-winged hawk travels long distances each year. He spends the summers as far north as Canada and he winters in the southern states of the United States even in South America.

You will know this hawk by its broad wings and short tail. The adult hawk has broad bars of color on its tail. He is about 15 inches long with a wingspread of about three feet, and he has powerful talons.

This friend to man is in danger of being destroyed by hunters. There are no laws to protect him yet.

1 Male; 2 Female

SCREECH OWL

THIS little owl doesn't screech at all. Instead it has a soft, sweet whistle. It is simple to imitate this whistle, and if you do, the owl will answer you!

The screech owl is a hunting bird, known as a bird of prey. These owls will attack and eat mice, young rabbits and rats, frogs, moths and other large insects, and also small birds. In turn, larger owls often attack and eat these screech owls.

The screech owl attacks mostly at night. During the day it is hard to see because of the way its colors blend into its surroundings.

Screech owls are found in all parts of the United States. They nest in the hollow parts of trees.

1 Adult; 2 and 3 Young

BLUE JAY

THE blue jay is one of the most intelligent and most colorful birds. He is found year-round in the eastern states and in southern Canada, west of the Rocky Mountains.

People have different ideas about whether or not the blue jay is helpful to man. In the picture at right you see the blue jay robbing a nest. He eats the eggs of other birds during the few short weeks of the nesting season each summer. For the rest of the year the blue jay eats small reptiles, mice and other rodents, grasshoppers, caterpillars, fruit-destroying beetles and other insects.

The jay is noted for its great boldness and noisy habits. Its call is a combination of loud screams, chatters and alarm cries mixed with softer notes.

1 Male; 2 and 3 Female

PILEATED WOODPECKER

THE pileated woodpecker is also called the "logcock." This bird is one of the largest of all woodpeckers. His bright red crest is lovely when he flies in the sunshine.

He has a long and powerful beak to peck at the bark of trees. The woodpecker pecks so that he can find the insects living in the trees and eat them. This is very helpful to the trees in the forest, because insects are destructive.

He is a shy bird. He seldom stays put when there are people around. Although he cannot be seen, he can be heard clearly as he pecks away at the trees.

These birds are found in the southern part of the United States.

1 Adult Male; 2 Adult Female; 3 and 4 Young Males

CATBIRD

THE catbird gets its name from its call, which sounds like a cat's meow. These birds nest in the United States, east of the Rocky Mountains, and are found all-year-round in Bermuda. They make themselves at home in city parks, in farmyards and in gardens.

The catbird can imitate many different sounds of other birds and animals. It is noted for its beautiful song, which it usually sings late at night.

This bird is a very helpful friend to man. It eats Japanese beetles and other insects that destroy land and food. The catbird also enjoys eating fruits and berries.

The catbird is about ten inches long. Its color is a dull gray and can be recognized by a patch of chestnut beneath its long tail.

1 Male; 2 Female

MEADOWLARK

THE meadowlark is one of the best loved of American birds because of its beautiful colors and its pretty song.

These birds build their nests out of grass on the ground in open fields such as golf courses or airports. The nests are out in the open, but the meadowlark is able to hide them so that they are hard to find.

Meadowlarks are good friends to the farmer. They eat worms, grasshoppers, caterpillars and other insects, as well as ragweed and other weed seeds.

Most birds hop when moving on the ground in search of food, but the meadowlark walks!

You will know the meadowlark by its bright gold breast with a black "V" coming down from the neck, and by its snow white outer tail feathers.

1 Males; 2 Females

26

27

CARDINAL

THE cardinal is easily recognized by its crest, the short feathers that grow on top of its head. The male cardinal (on the top branch in the picture) is a beautiful rich red color. Sometimes the cardinal is called the redbird.

This bird has a strong beak which makes it easy for him to crush the shells of seeds and nuts. Cardinals also like to eat sunflower seeds and insects.

The cardinal is one of the most popular American birds. One reason is its lovely appearance and another is its voice. The cardinal has a whistle that can be heard a mile away! It is not surprising that seven of the United States have named the cardinal as their state bird. These states are Illinois, Indiana, Kentucky, North Carolina, Ohio, Virginia and West Virginia.

Cardinals are found by swamps, woodlands and in gardens. They can be seen most often in the southern part of the United States.

1 Male; 2 Female

29

WOOD DUCK

No other waterfowl in the world can compare to the drake wood duck in beauty. He has bright, colorful feathers and is a very graceful bird. When the wood duck flies through the air, he looks just like a meteor falling through the sky.

This bird is called a wood duck because of its habit of living among woodland ponds and streams. The wood duck nests in hollow trees or branches.

The wood duck is found only in North America. It can be seen in practically every state in the United States and throughout most of Canada.

These beautiful birds have many enemies. Black snakes, opossums and raccoons kill a lot of the wood duck's eggs. Snapping turtles and large fish seize the ducklings and drag them into the deep waters to eat.

About fifty years ago these birds almost disappeared. Fortunately, the government made laws that limited the amount of wood ducks hunters could catch or shoot. Each year there are more and more wood ducks.

1 and 2 Males; 3 and 4 Females

GREAT BLUE HERON

THIS bird is about four feet tall, and its wings are six feet across when they are spread out. It flies with its long legs straight back, its neck curved, and its large wings flapping slowly and gracefully.

With its long, sharp beak, the great blue heron is an excellent fisher. He fishes for minnows, suckers and other small fish. He uses his beak as a spear when hunting mice, young rats, frogs and insects. He can even catch butterflies!

Great blue herons are found near ponds, marshes and riverbanks in Alaska, New York, Mexico, and Bermuda.

If the great blue heron is injured or crippled, you should stay away from it. The heron will stab with its beak at the eyes of any person or animal that comes near.

Male

MALLARD

THE mallard is sometimes called the "greenhead." It is one of the most abundant and important ducks in North America.

These ducks are popular with sportsmen and on the dinner table. In China, the meat and eggs of the mallard are very important items in the food supply.

You can tell the male mallard by its green head and white band around its neck. He also has white feathers in his tail. Mallards are seen in marshes, ponds, rivers and swamps.

These birds "quack" all the time. John James Audubon wrote that the mallard's cackling "would almost deafen you."

Mallards eat plants and are also fond of mosquitoes. They are found all over the United States and Canada.

The mallard is one of the fastest flying ducks in the world. They fly from forty-five to sixty miles per hour!

1 Males; 2 Females

BROWN PELICAN

JOHN James Audubon called the pelican "one of the most interesting of our American birds."

The pelican has a large and deep pouch under its beak. You cannot see it in this picture. Sometimes the mother or father pelican catches fish and keeps them in the pouch until he flies back to the nest. The baby pelican gets the fish by putting his head and neck into the parent bird's pouch and throat!

The pelican dives for the fish it feeds on. It dives from a height of fifteen or twenty feet above the water. It can catch as many as twenty fish in one dive!

In 1903, United States President Theodore Roosevelt created the first wild bird refuge, known as Pelican Island. This island protected these rare birds from hunters. There are now 270 refuges in existence.

The brown pelican is found along most of the southern coast of the United States.

Male Adult

ARCTIC TERN

THIS bird is known by its long fork-shaped tail and bright red feet and beak.

It is a seabird, and is usually found flying over the ocean. The picture at right shows the arctic tern ready to dive for fish. It flys with its beak pointed down and flaps its wings rapidly. When it sees a school of small fish it will dive into the water, grab one of the fish with its beak and fly back to shore with it.

Arctic terns are noisy birds. They give a loud and long cry when they want to sound an alarm.

The arctic tern flies almost the whole length of the world twice each year. In the summer the tern nests near the North Pole, and in Canada, Greenland, Europe and Siberia. In the winter it flies as far south as the Antarctic. The round-trip distance is 22,000 miles!

BLUE-WINGED TEAL

THE blue-winged teal is a small fresh-water duck. It can be found in swamps, marshes and ponds in the central United States and Canada.

Since these ducks fly and feed in large flocks, it is easy for hunters to spot them and shoot great numbers at one time. John James Audubon once saw a hunter fire two shots and bring down 94 blue-winged teals!

In recent years a large number of these blue-winged teals were killed when many of the swamps, and marshes in the United States were drained.

The male blue-winged teal has a white half-moon on his face. Both sexes have a large area of pale blue on the front of their wings.

These birds fly at a speed of about 50 miles an hour and travel further each year than any other American waterfowl.

1 Male; 2 Female

40

41

BAND-TAILED PIGEON

JOHN James Audubon never saw a band-tailed pigeon! He painted the picture at right from descriptions his friends gave him and from some pigeon skins.

These are rare birds. About fifty years ago, nearly all band-tailed pigeons were killed by hunters. This led to laws against killing these birds. Now there are many more band-tailed pigeons than there used to be.

Band-tailed pigeons need large forest areas to nest in. They eat nuts, berries and insects.

These pigeons are generally gray-blue, with a white half-moon on the back of the head. They have a wide band of bluff color at the end of a square tail. (Buff is a brownish yellow.)

When the band-tailed pigeon flies through the air, its wings make a noise like the sound of steam hissing from a kettle or radiator.

1 Male; 2 Female

TRUMPETER SWAN

THE trumpeter swan is the largest and heaviest of American wildfowl. This bird can spread its wings up to eight feet wide and it weighs *over* thirty pounds!

Because it is such a big bird, many hunters like to try to catch or shoot the trumpeter swan. When your grandparents were children, there were very few trumpeter swans left. But now these birds are protected by wardens and parks and it is against the law to shoot them. Every year more and more trumpeter swans appear.

Swans eat plants and grasses. With their long necks they dip down three feet or more into the water and nibble the stems and roots of water plants beneath the surface.

The trumpeter swan is found in Yellowstone Park and in Canada.

Adult

AMERICAN FLAMINGO

THE American flamingo is in danger of disappearing. The adults are still being killed for their gorgeous feathers and the young are hunted for food.

These birds live in the West Indies and along the coats of Yucatan and Brazil. Only an occasional wanderer will appear on the southern coast of Florida.

The flamingo uses its beak to scoop small shellfish from the floor of shallow waters. He plunges his head under water upside down, the upper bill serves as the scooper and the tongue serves as a sieve.

The American flamingo is a beautiful bird. Its coloring varies from rosy pink to pale orange. In captivity, flamingoes are purposely fed lots of carrots and carrot juices so that they can keep their lovely color.

Old Male

AUDUBON'S ANIMALS

WITH ILLUSTRATIONS BY
JOHN JAMES AUDUBON
AND
JOHN WOODHOUSE AUDUBON
WRITTEN BY
JAY BENNETT

THE GROLIER SOCIETY INC. • NEW YORK

OPOSSUM

AUDUBON called this little animal the Virginian opossum but it is also known as the Common opossum. Because the opossum has a pouch for carrying young, it is known as a marsupial. The opossum is the only marsupial to be found in all North America.

Baby opossums live in their mother's pouch for about ninety days. When they grow to the size of large mice they begin to venture out. They generally ride on their mother's back and sides. In a few more months they leave their mother's side and take on their own lives.

Opossums are tree climbers and they do most of their hunting at night. They seek small animals and insects. They also eat eggs and fruit, as well as berries.

When an opossum is threatened, he suddenly collapses. He plays "dead." The little animal just lies on the ground all curled up and motionless. That is where we get the expression to "play possum."

MOLE

MOLES like to make tunnels, so we may call them engineers of the animal world. They are small, tough creatures, with heavy and powerful shoulders. Their front legs are strong and wide, with heavy claws. These powerful front legs are used like shovels when the mole digs into the soft earth.

Most of a mole's life is spent underground. He is constantly digging in order to get the food he needs. He is a tremendous eater. The food he digs so much for are insects, beetles, and angle worms.

A mole has no visible ears and his eyes are either very small or absent. But he has a very sharp sense of touch. His sense of smell is also very keen. He grows to a length of seven inches.

It is very hard to believe the speed with which a mole works and the distance he can dig. In a single night a mole has been known to tunnel more than seventy-five yards.

SNOWSHOE RABBIT

AUDUBON called this animal the Northern hare. It is also known as the Snowshoe hare. Again, another name for it is the Varying hare. It is called "Varying" because its color changes from summer to winter.

The Snowshoe rabbit likes to be alone. He generally lives in northern forests and swamps. In the summer he is brown above and white below. In the winter he is white all over. When the snows come he blends in with the whiteness and is very hard to see.

He has large, long-furred feet which help him to travel over ice and snow. That is why he gets the name of Snowshoe rabbit.

He can jump along the ground with amazing speed. The Snowshoe rabbit can make five foot jumps at a time. Some naturalists say he can race along at a speed of 45 miles an hour.

In the summer the Snowshoe rabbit eats grass and plants. In the winter he chews the bark off young trees.

FOX SQUIRREL

THE Fox Squirrel is a big, husky fellow. In fact, he is the largest of all American tree squirrels. Some Fox squirrels are mostly rust-brown and tan. Others are grey and black. They generally grow to a length of over two feet.

Fox squirrels, Audubon called them Cat squirrels, live on the edge of forests. They are most common in the Southeastern part of the country. They like to eat nuts, seeds, fruit and berries. They are also very fond of acorns.

Some say they are lazy. If this is so, it is because they can defend themselves more easily from their enemies such as the hawks. They are not as fast-moving as most other squirrels. But they are pretty smart animals. When the Fox squirrel senses that danger is about, he will lie out on a tree limb and be completely unseen from below. Or he will vanish like a ghost in the forest about him.

WOODCHUCK

SOMETIMES you'll be walking along a field and the sun is high in a clear sky and suddenly you'll hear a shrill whistle.

The whistle of a woodchuck.

The woodchuck is also known by another name, he is called a groundhog. The woodchuck digs its burrow in a field or clearing. He eats clover and other plant foods all summer long. When autumn comes around, the woodchuck is pretty plump. With the coming of cold weather he ducks into his underground home. He generally stays there for the rest of the winter.

In many parts of the United States, February 2 is Groundhog Day. It is believed that on this day the groundhog comes out of his burrow and looks about. If he sees his shadow on the ground then he knows it's still winter. He hurries back into his shelter.

The woodchuck has many enemies. He is hunted by men, by hawks, coyotes, bears, and by foxes. He grows to a length of a little over two feet.

BLACK-TAILED
PRAIRIE DOG

T HE first thing to make sure about the Prairie Dog is that he is not a dog. He is a member of the squirrel family. This little animal got his name because he lived out on the Western prairie, wagged his tail and barked.

Prairie dogs are very social. They like to live together in colonies that are called Prairie Dog towns. A little over a half a century ago there were still many large prairie dog towns in the West. One naturalist tells of a prairie dog town that was 250 miles long and 100 miles wide. He believed that more than four hundred million prairie dogs lived in this vast community.

Prairie dogs feed mainly on grass and other green plants. They sit by their little earth mounds and sun themselves. At the first sign of danger they give a shrill whistle and vanish into the earth.

PORCUPINE

For a long time people thought that a porcupine shoots his quills. In fact, there are some people who still think so. They believe that when the porcupine is attacked he turns his back to his enemy, and then fires away. But this is not so.

What happens is this: The animal does turn, and then he lashes out with his tail, which is covered with spines, or quills. These quills, which are loosely attached to the back and tail of the porcupine, penetrate the body of the attacker. It should be remembered that there are about thirty thousand quills covering the porcupine.

Porcupines live mainly in forests. They generally come out at night. Porcupines eat leaves, buds, and they gnaw away at the bark of trees. They cause great damage to trees.

RED FOX

HE has very good hearing. He depends more on this than on his sight when he is being hunted. The Red Fox, or Cross Fox as Audubon calls him, is one of the most cunning of all animals. He is found in many parts of the continent. His fur is valuable and is much used by women for scarves and coats.

The Red Fox is sometimes mistaken for a small dog or a coyote. But the best way to single him out is to look at his tail. The Red Fox has a tail that is tipped with white hairs. In the winter time he does not have a den, but sleeps out in the open. He curls himself up and covers his nose and paws with his bushy tail. That's how he keeps his nose and paws from freezing.

When he is hunted, the Red Fox is just full of tricks. Many a hunter comes back from the chase with a foolish grin on his face. The Red Fox has outsmarted him.

COYOTE

ANYBODY who has read some Western stories, or has seen cowboy movies, surely knows what a coyote looks like. This animal is as much a part of the Great West as the steer and range grass are. His high-pitched cry at night is known throughout cowboy land.

The Coyote has another name; he is often called the Prairie Wolf. He is about four and a half feet long and weighs about 26 pounds. Coyotes are found all over North America, from Alaska down.

For a long time, man has waged war on the coyote. He has killed off very many of these Prairie Wolves. But there are naturalists who claim that this is all wrong. They point out that Coyotes feed on destructive rabbits and rodents. They help protect grass that cattle need for grazing.

The life span of a coyote is about 14 years.

GRAY WOLF

AUDUBON called this fierce animal that he painted, the White American Wolf. But he is far better known as the Gray Wolf. Many Gray Wolves are all white as this one is, others are black. But most of these animals are grayish in color all year long.

Gray Wolves are huge and fierce. They grow as long as 7 feet. They can weigh as much as 150 pounds. At one time the Gray Wolf was found nearly all over the United States. The pioneers told of many exciting experiences with Gray Wolves. But today, except for some few areas, it is hard to come across a Gray Wolf.

He is also called the Timber Wolf. Living mostly in Canada and Alaska, this animal hunts alone or in packs. He attacks deer, sheep, cattle and horses. The life span of the Gray Wolf is up to 15 years.

BLACK BEAR

He stands on his hind legs like a man, and he can be very friendly. He is nice to watch when he is in a cage in the zoo. The American Black Bear, as Audubon called him, can give you a lot of fun.

But should you be out in one of our national parks and come across a Black Bear, be sure to leave him alone. Because any animal that weighs up to 400 pounds and is about six feet in length, has big claws and teeth, can be very dangerous.

The Black Bear can do a lot of things. He can climb trees quite easily, he can move along the ground quite rapidly, and he can swim in water for five miles or even further. He is both a vegetarian and a meat eater, He likes fish, honey and spends a good deal of his time hunting wild berries.

Black Bears live in forests, by swamps and in mountain areas.

LONG-TAILED WEASEL

AUDUBON called this animal the Little Nimble Weasel. Most naturalists prefer to name it the Long-Tailed Weasel. As far as its being nimble, Audubon was quite right. The Long-Tailed Weasel is one of the quickest of all animals. His movements are sharp and lightning-like. He is bold and fierce. Cornered weasels have been known to savagely attack men.

The Weasel keeps to himself and generally likes to hunt at night. However, he has been seen out at day. The Weasel hunts mice, rats, birds and will even spring on rabbits and chickens. The owl and the eagle are the bitter enemies of the Weasel.

The Long-Tailed Weasel is brown in the summer but in the winter, especially in the north, he becomes white. His tail is tipped with black.

Weasels are found in most parts of the United States and in some areas of Mexico and Canada. The Long-Tailed Weasel grows to a length of two feet.

MINK

AUDUBON in this painting shows two of the animals together. However, it is rare that this is so. Most Minks are solitary creatures. They like to keep to themselves and to hunt by themselves.

The Mink is at home both on land and in water. He swims and dives with great skill. In the water, where he spends a good deal of his time, he hunts for fish, frogs or crayfish. He can dive twenty feet deep and can swim more than a hundred feet underwater. He can do all this because his hind feet are webbed.

In the winter time, the Mink will get a bit away from his water home and concentrate on the land. He will then hunt rabbits for food.

Mink fur is very valuable and is made into expensive fur coats. Today thousands of Minks are raised on fur farms, or Mink Ranches as they are called.

BADGER

You can tell a Badger by looking at its white stripe. The broad stripe runs like a ribbon from nose to back over the top of the animal's head. The Badger is small, measuring less than three feet from nose to tail. But there are very few animals that will take him on in battle.

He is as tough as they come. Badgers have killed dogs and coyotes a good deal larger than they were. They have strong teeth and claws and they hiss and snarl and just stand their ground. Any man facing an angry Badger had better have a gun in his two hands.

Badgers like to roam the open country and to dig into the earth for prairie dogs. They also hunt ground squirrels, snakes, birds, and love to eat eggs. Badgers live in deep burrows which they make for themselves. During the winter they get into their dens and sleep away.

OTTER

H E loves to play. But he likes best of all to slide. To slide down a path he has made and into the water, making a big splash. Then to make his way out of the water, up to the top of the runway, and then down again. In the winter time he will be seen sliding down a hill that is white with sparkling snow. The Otter is a fun-loving animal that likes to be with its kind, tumbling, wrestling, and sliding. He is ever active, sometimes travelling as much as fifty miles from his home.

Otters are excellent swimmers and are generally found near streams, lakes and rivers. The Otter that Audubon painted is called a River Otter. Audubon called him the Canada Otter. These furry animals feed on fish, frogs, turtles and at times muskrats and beavers.

They grow to about five feet long and weigh up to 30 pounds. They range through most of the United States, but are not found in some areas of the Southwest.

COUGAR

THIS animal has many names. It has been called the panther, the mountain lion, the puma and the painter. Our pioneers told many tales of the scream of the painter at night. They said that the scream sounded like that of a woman in great fright and pain. But though the Cougar can sound terrifying, and though he can appear terrifying, he has rarely been known to attack man. In fact, some naturalists say that he never has.

Cougars are the biggest cats in this country. They grow as much as nine feet long and have weighed up to 250 pounds. In colonial days there were quite a lot of Cougars roaming the forests of the East. Today there are very few left. Most are in the western part of the United States.

The main prey of the Cougar is the deer. The Cougar will hunt for many miles without resting. He is very powerful and with one spring can bring down a big deer.

DEER

THE Deer is one of the most-loved of all animals. He is so gentle, has such soft eyes, moves with such grace, that it is a delight to look at him. Beautiful poems and lovely stories have been written about Deer. Audubon painted this picture of the White-tailed Deer with great tenderness. He called this quiet being the Common American Deer.

White-tailed Deer stand about 4 feet high and are close to 7 feet long. They weigh up to 350 pounds. These animals range throughout most of the United States. Because they have been protected by law, the White-tailed Deer have grown in great numbers. In some areas they have become a severe problem.

This is so because Deer are browsers. They feed on leaves, twigs, and fruits. They destroy forest trees, crops of farmers and ruin orchards. When they come out at night and cross highways, they are a great danger to drivers of automobiles.

It is a problem that will have to be solved.

MOOSE

HE is big and ugly looking, and he can be pretty fierce when he is angered. Moose have been known to charge at men and send them running for shelter. Even bears do their best to get out of the way of an enraged Moose.

The Moose is the largest of all American deer. At his shoulders he can be as much as 7 feet high and can weigh over 1500 pounds. The male Moose, who is called a Bull Moose, has huge flat antlers that may spread to 6 feet from tip to tip.

Moose can be found in Alaska, Canada and some of the northern states of this country. They are fine swimmers. A Moose can swim ten miles across water. These huge animals like to live in forests and generally near lakes.

Moose like to wade into a shallow lake and eat water lilies and other plants that grow in water. They also eat herbs and twigs.

AMERICAN BISON

H E is better known as the Buffalo, but his true name is the American Bison. The Bison is the largest American animal. He is huge. Bison measure up to 11 feet long and stand 6 feet high at the shoulder. Their weight is enormous, some bison weigh close to 3,000 pounds.

It is tragic when one looks back a bit on the history of this giant. Just a few hundred years ago there were some 60 million Bison on this continent. In 1889 a count was made —only 541 of these animals were left in the United States. Some naturalists claim that the count was even lower.

The Bison, or Buffalo, was simply destroyed. He was killed off by hunters and by people who didn't care too much about the future of this American animal. But conservationists, people who care about animals and forests, were finally able to save the Buffalo.

Today, the number of Bison in the United States is about 6,000.

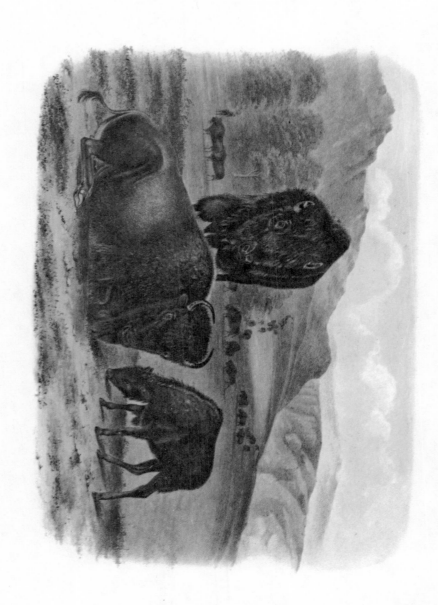

MOUNTAIN GOAT

In the summer time he lives high up in the mountains. This white, shaggy animal is at home in the rocky heights. He bounds along from crag to crag with grace and ease. He stands poised at the edge of a cliff, a thrilling sight to see. Then he will make an amazing leap through space and land safely on a projecting rock.

Audubon called him the Rocky Mountain Goat. But most naturalists refer to him as a Goat-Antelope.

The Mountain Goat seeks his food among the scattered rocks. He eats the grass that grows there. In the winter he will come down from his rocky land.

Mountain Goats weigh up to 300 pounds and are about five feet long. They never change color, remaining white throughout the four seasons. Their chief enemies are bears, foxes, cougars and wolves.

SKUNK

THE painting of this beautiful animal with its uplifted tail was done by one of Audubon's sons, John Woodhouse Audubon. He came across this small, alert-looking fellow while on an expedition in Texas in the winter of 1845. John Audubon called this animal a large-tailed skunk. Today, it is more generally known as the hooded skunk.

Hooded skunks are found in southwestern United States all the way down to Central America. They love to run in woods, along plains and in desert areas.

Even though skunks give off a terribly bad smell when threatened, they are usually very mild animals. Skunks help farmers all over the country. They eat great quantities of insects and their grubs. They also eat rodents and other small animals, as well as fruit and berries.

Most skunks are about the size of house cats. They raise from four to six young in a season.

44

JOHN JAMES AUDUBON

JOHN JAMES AUDUBON was born on his father's plantation in Les Cayes, Santo Domingo, in 1785. His father took him to Paris where he studied with the great French painter, Jacques Louis David. This was the only training that he ever got as an artist.

At the age of 17 Audubon came to the United States. At the age of 23 he was married. From then on, Audubon spent the best part of his life painting birds and animals. In 1838 he published his *Birds of America*, which is known to this day as one of the finest works on the subject.

He was working on a book of paintings of the animals of North America when he died. His sons finished the work.

The Audubon Society for nature lovers is named after this great painter and naturalist.

John James Audubon died in 1851.